The Glider Trial Flight Guide

Congratulations!

This is your first step into the wonderful
World of Aviation.

Your personal invitation to experience the
pleasure of being airborne.

Ken Stewart

Nothing in this manual supersedes any legislation, rules, regulations or procedures contained in any operational document issued by Her Majesty's Stationery Office, the Civil Aviation Authority, the Joint Aviation Authorities, ICAO, the manufacturers of aircraft, engines and systems, or by the operators of aircraft throughout the world.

The Glider Trial Flight Guide - Ken Stewart

Copyright 2007 © Pooleys Flight Equipment Ltd

First Edition 2007

ISBN 978-1-84336-095-7

Pooleys Flight Equipment Ltd
Elstree Aerodrome
Hertfordshire
WD6 3AW
England

Tel: 0208 953 4870
Fax: 0208 953 2512
www.pooleys.com

Ken Stewart started gliding in 1972 on a 5-day holiday course in the Cairngorm Mountains in Scotland. It was just one of several sports that he intended trying that year, as leave from work permitted.

The weather was disappointing and allowed only a few short 5-minute flights – except for the last flight that lasted 30 minutes. On that flight, the glider soared among the most majestic mountains in Britain, giving views unimagined by most of the population busy with their daily toils on the ground.

The next week was spent canoeing but the following weekend found him back at the Cairngorm Gliding Club. One flight and he was "hooked".

Ken qualified as an instructor in 1976 and soon took up gliding instruction as a profession at the Lasham Gliding Centre *(reputedly the largest gliding centre in the world)*. After a few years, he became Deputy Chief Flying Instructor and, for a period, Acting Chief Flying Instructor. In 1981, he became British National Coach, a post that he held for six years before deciding on a change of career – to become an airline pilot.

He is now a captain on Boeing 737s but still believes that gliding is "the most beautiful way to fly".

He is also the author of THE GLIDER PILOT'S MANUAL and THE SOARING PILOT'S MANUAL.

Enjoy your Glider Trial Flight – but beware – it could change your life. Ken will vouch for that.

Editors

Dorothy Pooley

Dorothy is an instructor and examiner with over 7000 hours, who runs fixed wing flying instructor courses at Shoreham. She is also a CAA Flight Instructor Examiner and holds a commercial helicopter licence.

Daljeet Gill

Daljeet is Head of Design & Development for Pooleys Flight Equipment. Editor of the Pooleys Private Pilots Guides by David Cockburn, Pre-flight Briefing (Aeroplanes & Helicopters), R/T Communications, Pooleys JAR Manuals plus many others. Daljeet has been involved with editing, typesetting and design for these publications. Graduated in 1999 with a BA (hons) in Graphic Design, she deals with marketing, advertising & design of our new products. She maintains our website and produces our Pooleys Catalogue annually.

Acknowledgments

This guide would not have been possible without the help and support of the London Gliding Club and Lasham Gliding Society. The author is extremely grateful to both these organisations and also to Mark Taylor for allowing the use of his illustrations. Thanks go to Diana Bartlett for applying her proof-reading skills.

Introduction

Whether or not the Glider Trial Flight you are about to take was a gift or your own idea, you will find your enjoyment of the experience will be enhanced if you read through this short introductory guide in advance of your flight.

This guide is written only as an introduction to the gliding experience and, as such, it is not necessary to learn and remember the contents. Its aims are merely to describe what you can expect and to prepare you so that you can fully enjoy your day's gliding.

On the day of your Glider Trial Flight, your instructor will explain all you need to know and will be glad to answer any queries you may have.

Have a good flight.

Contents

Your Glider Flight

A little bit of Technical Stuff

Your Glider Trial Flight

So you've decided to have a Glider Trial Flight. Or perhaps it wasn't your idea! There are many ways your Glider Trial Flight may have been arranged.

It may have been a gift from a friend or relation who has given you a Glider Trial Flight Voucher. These are available from some gliding clubs, the British Gliding Association and in many "*Adventure Experience*" packages sold commercially from high street stores or on the internet.

Alternatively, your flight may have been arranged directly with a gliding club. In this case, no voucher may have been issued, but a "*booking*" for the flight will have been made – usually by telephone.

You may have simply turned up at a gliding club and arranged the trial flight personally – perhaps even for the same day.

By whichever method your trial flight was arranged, it will have been made clear to you what you will be entitled to, either verbally, written on the voucher or in the literature enclosed in your "*Adventure Experience*" package. This will vary depending on which gliding club you fly from.

There are good reasons for this. The main factor is the facilities used to launch the glider into the air.

If the glider is towed into the air behind a light aircraft *(a technique known as "aerotowing")* then the glider can be towed up to a desired height before the glider is released to start gliding flight. When aerotowing is used, your Glider Trial Flight will normally involve a launch to 2,000 or possibly 3,000 feet above the airfield, followed by a flight lasting from around 15 to 20 minutes.

If, on the other hand, the gliding club launches its gliders into the air using a winch or car launch system, then the height typically achieved will be just over 1,000 feet and the flight time around 5 minutes. In this instance, the Glider Trial Flight scheme may consist of 2 or 3 flights or a guaranteed total time in the air.

Not all gliding sites have aerotow facilities. Some only have winch *(or car)* launching available while some sites have both.

Your Glider Trial Flight will also include a briefing on the gliding operation and the glider. This will include all the relevant safety matters as well as points that will add to your comfort and enjoyment of the experience.

Also included may be added bonuses, such as membership of the gliding club for a period *(often 28 days)* which will allow you to have other training flights at the same rates that club members pay.

There will also be other gliding club members on the airfield, out enjoying their sport. You will be encouraged to join in and help them at the launch point. Gliding is a non-professional sport where everyone gets involved, thus keeping the costs down and adding to the camaraderie. Don't hesitate to ask these enthusiasts any questions you have. It's all part of the Glider Trial Flight experience.

What does a Glider flight involve?

A glider trial flight is not a passenger flight or a sightseeing trip in a glider. It is an instructional flight designed not only to let you experience how pleasant it is like to fly in a glider, but also to show you how easy a glider is to control. Its aim is to give you a chance to see if you fancy taking up gliding as a sport.

You will fly in a two-seat glider with an instructor who is trained to the standards laid down by the British Gliding Association.

The flight will begin with the instructor flying the glider during the launch and for a period after the launch. During this part of the flight, local landmarks — towns, lakes, motorways, etc. will be pointed out to you. This is a good time to take photographs if you wish.

Although he or she will be in charge of the flight throughout, during the higher part of the flight and depending on time available, the instructor may demonstrate the three primary controls: the elevator, the ailerons and the rudder. After each demonstration, you will have the opportunity to try each of these controls for yourself.

After you have tried each of the primary controls, your instructor will demonstrate how to turn the glider before again giving you control so that you can have a go.

If you have been launched by aerotow then you may have time to practise several turns before the instructor once again takes control.

If, on the other hand, a winch has launched the glider then it may take two or three launches to gain enough time in the air to achieve all of these demonstrations.

As the glider gradually loses height, your instructor will be flying the glider into a position from where the final approach to the landing can be made. Now you can just sit back and enjoy the view. This is another superb time to take photographs.

Gliding in the UK

Gliding in the United Kingdom is governed by the British Gliding Association *(BGA)*, which operates under the auspices of the Civil Aviation Authority.

The BGA consists of approximately 10,000 members who fly from the 100 or so gliding clubs dotted around the country. All civilian gliding in the UK takes place from these clubs. *(There is also a different system of gliding clubs for military personnel.)*

The clubs vary in size. A few have 400 or more members but some have less than 100. The members of a gliding club will be responsible for the club's operation. This depends on volunteers to carry out more or less all the tasks required to keep the gliders flying. Such tasks will include instructing, operating the launch equipment, repositioning gliders after landing, etc. as well as all of the management roles. All this teamwork leads to a very friendly atmosphere where everyone helps everyone else.

The Gliding Site

Just like gliding clubs, gliding sites vary immensely in both size and operation. Often the gliding site may be an active or disused airfield. Many clubs operate from a farmer's field or an area of level heath land. Irrespective of size or venue, all clubs operate to the high safety standards required by the BGA.

The number of gliders operating from a club will also vary. This fleet will normally be made up of several club-owned gliders and many that are privately owned by members. All of the training will be done in the club's two-seat gliders. If the club uses light aircraft to tow the gliders into the air, then usually the club will also own these.

Weather permitting, some of the larger clubs operate seven days a week throughout the year, while others only operate at weekends and on public holidays, as well as specific midweek days. A few will have a small number of professional staff, but most rely on the skills of their members.

Before you set off to the Gliding Site

Although your Glider Trial Flight voucher may be valid for some considerable time *(if indeed there is a limit on it at all)* you have probably arranged to take your flight on a specific day. When that day arrives, it is best to contact the gliding club before setting off to make sure that weather conditions are suitable for your flight.

The club's aim is to give you the best possible introduction to the sport. With that in mind, they will not want you to go away disappointed if the flight was conducted in inappropriate weather. Although the weather may appear pleasant enough at your home, it may not be as pleasant at the gliding club if this is some distance away or is in an exposed situation.

By contacting the club before you depart, they can advise you if it is too windy, too misty or the cloud is too low for your flight. Such advice will save you time and petrol, and means that you can enjoy the gliding experience more on another day. If the weather appears to you to be too gloomy, then by contacting them, you will be able to confirm this and arrange another day.

Lastly, it is unwise to fly if you feel unwell. Simple things like a head cold or upset stomach can ruin the trial flight experience. A head cold can cause problems by blocking sinuses, or cause pain and even damage to your eardrums as the air pressure changes as the glider descends. If in doubt, call the gliding club and postpone your flight to another day. They will understand.

What to Wear

At the gliding club, nothing runs to a schedule. That's what makes it relaxing.

Don't be surprised if you have to wait for your flight. Probably the glider will be in flight on a training exercise when you arrive and you will have to wait for it to land. Even then, you might have to wait in a queue of other gliders for the launch. There will be a lot going on, such as gliders launching, landing and soaring overhead. Just relax and enjoy the atmosphere.

This waiting time can be useful as it gives your instructor time to explain the operation and tell you a bit about your flight.

However, your time spent at the launch area will be out in the open air. This means you must dress wisely for the conditions. If it is a lovely summer's day then light summer clothing, with maybe a light jacket, is fine. On a windy day you will need to dress as if you were going hill walking with enough clothes to keep out the cold.

You may be walking around on wet grass or muddy areas, and light boots or strong shoes are an advantage.

Ladies should wear trousers or jeans as skirts make getting into and out of gliders difficult and may also restrict movement of the glider's controls.

Once in the glider you will be warmer – either due to the sun warming you through the Perspex canopy or as a result of being out of the wind. Your instructor will tell you if he or she thinks that you are likely to be too warm, so that you can shed some layers of clothing if necessary.

In summer, you would be wise to wear a small sun hat and some protection against sunburn. Sunglasses are a must on bright days.

Dress comfortably. Don't worry about fashion – no one else will.

At the Airfield

When you arrive at the gliding site, the first thing to do is to ask one of the club members where you should check in. Some gliding clubs are too small to have an office that serves as a reception. However, there will be some focal point where you can do the necessary paperwork and be introduced to your instructor.

The main thing at this stage is not to stray onto any part of the airfield where aircraft or gliders are manoeuvring. For safety, introduce yourself to any club member and tell them that you are there for a Glider Trial Flight. They will point you in the right direction and will probably escort you to the office or the launch point.

Once you find the right place, be it an office, the clubhouse or the launch point control van, you will be asked to fill in some forms. These are legally required for insurance purposes and will only take a few minutes to complete.

Safety

For your safety, it is important that you stay away from the various aircraft and vehicles that are constantly moving around the airfield, unless you are escorted.

Occasionally, the club member with you may have to go and help to retrieve or launch a glider. You might be invited to help, but if not, you are best to stay at the place where other club members are congregating. This is usually close to the launch control van.

In addition to the above, here are a few notes that will help you to stay safe on the airfield:

- *never touch aircraft propellers.*
- *when crossing any open areas, keep a good lookout – a glider may be landing on the area you want to cross and you won't hear it coming.*
- *towing aircraft trail a long rope with metal rings on its end when they land – so although the aeroplane may be well above you as they pass, the rope and rings may be lower and closer to you than you expect.*
- *never walk in front of a glider at the launch point – it may have a launch cable attached and be about to launch.*
- *never touch or stand near launch cables that are lying on the ground.*

The launch point is where it all happens.

It is here that the gliders are lined up to await a launch. Close by, other gliders will be parked while their pilots inspect and prepare them for flight. Some gliders may still be in the process of being assembled, having been kept in purpose-built trailers overnight.

As well as helping to launch gliders, other club members will be keeping a log of the flights, signalling to start the launch of gliders, driving tractors to fetch launch cables after a glider launch or retrieving gliders that have landed.

Instructors will be briefing and debriefing students before and after flights. The launch point is probably where you will be introduced to your instructor and the glider you will fly.

The Launch Point

At the Glider

By the time your instructor starts to show you around the glider, you will probably have observed gliders being launched and landing.

Now your instructor will tell you a bit more about the glider you will fly, and start preparing you for your flight.

You may be given a parachute to wear. Don't worry. Although this is a fully serviceable parachute, wearing it is only a precaution against the unlikely event that your glider should collide with another aircraft. Since most glider seats are designed for a pilot who is wearing a parachute, it is also necessary if you are to be comfortable. You will be shown how to don the parachute and how you would use it.

You will be shown how to get into your seat in the cockpit and how to secure the seat harness. If you are smaller or taller than average, the seat and/or the rudder pedals can be adjusted so that you can operate all of the controls easily.

All of the various controls, knobs, levers and instruments will be shown to you, as well what they do or display.

Your instructor will describe how the flight you are about to take will be conducted, giving you an idea of what you can expect to see and the sensations you will feel.

Once you are seated and strapped in, your instructor will carry out a series of pre-flight checks to make sure everything is ready for the launch. After these are complete, the launch cable or towrope will be attached and the launch will begin.

All you have to do is sit back and enjoy your Glider Trial Flight.

The Flight Itself

The Launch *(by Aerotow)*

The launch begins with the glider running along the ground at increasing speed as it is towed behind a light aircraft. After a short ground run the glider will take off – sometimes before the towing aircraft gets airborne. Your instructor's aim is now to keep the glider low until the towing aircraft gets off the ground and into the air.

Once the aircraft and glider combination is airborne, all that is required is for the glider to follow the towplane around the sky until the glider reaches the height at which your instructor will release the towrope.

The aerotow launch can take five or six minutes to complete. You will have time to enjoy the view.

The Aerotow Launch

The Launch (by Winch or Car)

The launch begins with a much quicker acceleration than on an aerotow launch. The ground run is very short. As soon as the glider is airborne, it climbs at an increasingly steep angle until it is climbing at its optimum attitude with the nose pointing upwards.

As the glider reaches the top of the launch, the instructor will lower the glider's nose and release the launch cable.

The whole launch is over in less than a minute.

The Winch Launch

After Release

After the towrope or launch cable is released, the glider is now in gliding flight.

Your instructor will show you where the airfield is and show you the local landmarks and area. If you are from a nearby town, ask the instructor to point this out to you. It can be fascinating to see a place you know from the air.

Once you have become accustomed to being airborne in a glider, your instructor will show you the effect of each of the main controls. After each demonstration you will be able to try each control for yourself.

If time permits *(or perhaps on a second or third flight if launched by winch or car)* your instructor will demonstrate other effects of the controls before showing you how to turn the glider. After this, you will be able to try a few turns.

During this time, the glider will have been slowly descending and your instructor will position the glider for the landing.

With the glider lined up with the airfield, your instructor will be able to fly it down the approach path and land.

During the approach to land, your instructor will normally open the airbrakes. These are designed to assist the pilot to land the glider at the desired position on the airfield. Depending on the type of glider, using the airbrakes will cause a slight "rumbling". This is normal and nothing to worry about.

Just before the glider reaches the ground, your instructor will reduce the glider's rate of descent, resulting in the glider settling gently onto the ground.

Once on the ground the glider will roll a short way before coming to a stop.

The Glider

Normally, the glider in which you will fly on your Glider Trial Flight will be one of the gliding club's training gliders. Whether it is made from wood and fabric, metal or fibreglass, it will be maintained to the high standards required by the British Gliding Association.

Obviously, it will have two seats. Occasionally, these seats will be "side-by-side" but more commonly, they will be arranged one behind the other. If you do fly in such a "tandem" glider, you will normally fly in the front seat with your instructor seated behind you. This will give you a better view and is also the seat you will occupy should you decide to continue your training - and indeed when you "go solo" when your initial training programme is complete.

Both of the seating positions are equipped with a full set of controls and instruments. Communication between you and your instructor can be carried out in a normal way without the need for headsets – such is the relative quietness of a glider's cockpit.

Many people think that gliders are frail and flimsy machines. In fact, gliders are designed to be strong enough to take loads equal to or greater that most light powered aircraft. Most are cleared to do aerobatics and all have the same primary controls as airliners.

ASK 13   2-seater glider

ASK 21   glass-fibre 2-seater glider

The Main Parts of the Glider

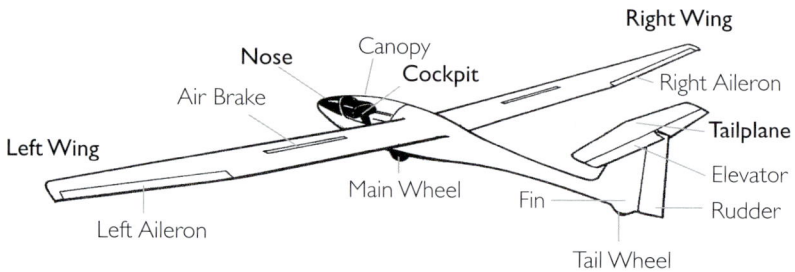

The Cockpit

The glider's cockpit is the "*control room*" of the glider. As well as having the seats for the pilots it also contains all of the control levers and instruments you need when flying the glider. Here is a brief description of the main controls.

A modern glider cockpit, showing the control column *(near centre)*, instrument panel, airbrake lever *(left side)* and cable release knob *(in front of airbrake lever)*.

The Control Column

The control column *(or "stick")* is the main control. Put simply, you move the control column in the direction you want the glider's nose to point, left or right, up or down. This is how you turn the glider, or decrease or increase speed.

The Rudder Pedals

The rudder pedals are used to deflect the rudder. Pressing on the left ruddr pedal moves the rudder to the left and pressing on the right rudder pedal moves the rudder to the right. They also steer the glider when it is rolling along the ground before take-off and after landing.

The Airbrake Lever

The airbrake lever *(always painted blue)* is used to extend and retract the airbrake paddles on the wing. These control the glider's rate of descent so that you can land exactly where you want.

The Trim Lever

The trim lever *(always painted green)* usually referred to simply as the *"trimmer"*, is used to remove the control forces on the control column so that you don't have to push or pull constantly on the control column when flying the glider straight at a steady speed.

The Tow Cable Release Knob

The tow cable release knob *(always painted yellow)* is attached to the hook mechanism that holds the towrope or launch cable to the glider during the take-off. When you get to the top of the launch, pulling on this knob releases the glider from the tow and you can begin to glide and soar like a bird.

Other Controls

The cockpit will include other control levers and knobs. These will vary depending on the glider. These include such controls as mechanisms to open and close the cockpit canopy, wheel brake levers, seat adjustments, etc.

The Instruments

At first sight, the instrument array on some gliders can look complicated. However, there are only three instruments that need to be considered by an early student. For this reason, many training gliders have instrument panels that contain only the basic instruments required. So don't be concerned if the instrument panel has fewer instruments than you would see on a powered aeroplane.

Instrument panel, showing *(left to right)*
Top row - airspeed indicator and electric variometer,
Middle row - compass, accelerometer, turn and slip indicator, thermal averager, variometer
Bottom of panel - altimeter

The Airspeed Indicator

This shows how fast the glider is flying through the air *(its AIRSPEED)*.

As the glider's control and handling depend upon the glider's speed through the air, this is an important instrument.

The Airspeed Indicator (ASI)

This indicates how high the glider is flying relative to a reference height. On local training flights it is usually set to tell the height of the glider above the airfield.

The altimeter normally has three needles *(or pointers)* which are read like the hands of a clock. The large needle indicates 100s of feet, while the next largest needle indicates 1,000s of feet. So when the large needle passes 999 feet, the next largest needle would point at the 1 on the dial, indicating 1,000 feet. The smallest needle behaves the same for 10,000s of feet.

The small digital scale is used for setting the reference height and can be ignored at this stage.

The Altimeter

The Variometer

This shows the rate at which the glider is climbing or descending. Aeroplane pilots call this type of instrument a "*vertical speed indicator*".

As the whole aim of gliding is to find currents of air that are rising fast enough to keep the glider airborne, this is probably the most important instrument in the glider. So much so, in fact, that gliders with a large number of instruments will often have more than one type of variometer on their instrument panels.

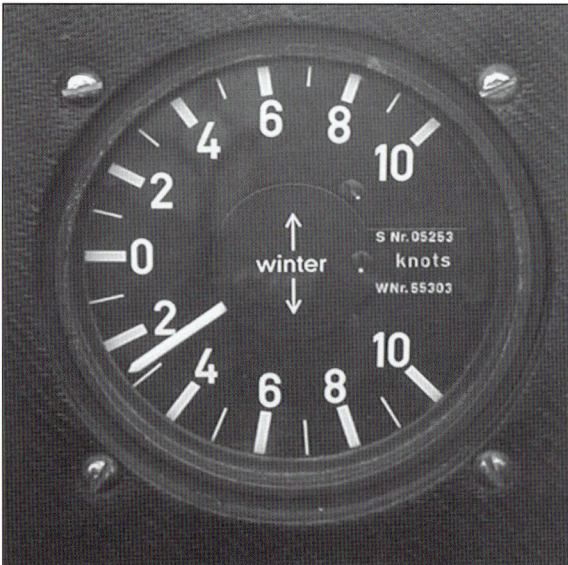

The Variometer

How a Glider Flies

Gravity & Weight

Everything is affected by gravity. It's what makes apples fall from trees. It's what stops us from floating off into space. Its effect also gives us our weight.

In many ways, weight is annoying. An object's weight may make it difficult to lift. Even worse, it's so persistent that it took us a long time to defeat it and take to the air.

WEIGHT is a force that acts on everything. It always acts vertically downwards.

For an aeroplane or a glider to be able to fly, we need to create a force that is at least equal to weight but which acts upwards. Once we have created that force, we call it **LIFT**.

Lift

Both aeroplanes and gliders *(in this aspect they are the same)* create the force we call **LIFT** because they have wings.

Apart from being a long, thin structure relative to the rest of the aircraft, the wing is a very special shape. If you sliced the wing open by sawing it vertically downwards you would see that the wing, rather than being a flat structure, is curved, the top surface of the wing being more curved than the bottom surface.

As the wing moves forwards through the air, this shape has an effect on the air that creates the force we require – that is **LIFT**.

Briefly this is how it works:

- As the air meets the forward edge of the wing, some of it will flow over the top of the wing and some of it flows under the wing. The wing has a strange effect on the air. The curved top of the wing causes the air passing over it to speed up relative to the air going under the wing's flatter bottom surface. This causes a reduction in the pressure of the air above the wing.

- This has the effect of sucking the wing upwards. In other words, we have created a force that acts upwards. This force is **LIFT**. The airflow over its upper surface produces approximately two thirds of the **LIFT** a wing creates. The airflow past the lower surface produces the remainder.

- If we can make this force large enough it will counter **WEIGHT** and the aircraft will fly.

(If this sounds implausible, take a sheet of paper and hold it by the corners at one edge so that it curves downwards away from you. Now blow over the top curved surface and you will see the paper wants to rise.)

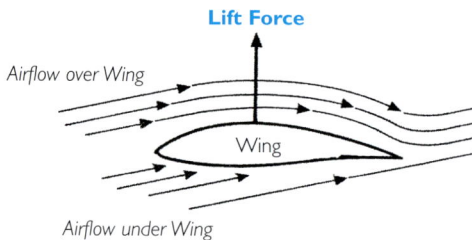

Creation of Lift

Aeroplanes versus Gliders

Before the wing will produce **LIFT** to counter the aircraft's weight, it has to move forward through the air. With an aeroplane, this is achieved by using the engine to pull or push the aircraft through the air.

After launch, a glider, not having an engine, moves through the air by tilting the **LIFT** force forwards.

In fact, this tilting of the **LIFT** force is also used to turn the glider. This is why aeroplanes and gliders always bank their wings when turning.

The Controls & What they Do?

Once you are airborne and the glider has released the rope attaching it to the towing aircraft, your instructor will demonstrate how the primary controls work and what their effect is on the glider's flight. You will also be shown how to turn the glider. The following notes may help you understand better what your instructor is demonstrating when in flight.

There are three main controls on the glider: the **ELEVATOR**, the **AILERONS** and the **RUDDER**.

The Elevator

The elevator is a horizontal control surface at the rear of the glider and is attached by hinges to the tailplane so that it can be moved up and down relative to the tailplane. It is controlled by moving the control column backwards *(elevator moves up)* and forwards *(elevator moves down)*.

Normally, the glider is flown by referring to the view over the nose of the glider and the amount of ground in view. The position of the glider's nose relative to the horizon is known as the glider's <u>attitude</u>.

Moving the control column forwards lowers the glider's nose relative to the horizon. More ground can be seen over the glider's nose and the glider flies faster.

Moving the control column backwards raises the glider's nose relative to the horizon. Less ground can be seen over the glider's nose and the glider flies slower.

Normal Gliding Attitude

Note the amount of ground in view over the glider's nose.

Move Control Column **Forward**

Glider's nose goes down more ground in view airspeed increases.

Move Control Column **Back**

Glider's nose comes up less ground in view airspeed decreases.

The ailerons are two control surfaces – one attached to the rear of each of the glider's wings. Each aileron is hinged to its respective wing so that it can be moved up and down relative to the wing.

The ailerons are connected to the control column in such a way that when the control column is moved sideways *(to the left or right)* one aileron will move upwards while the other moves downwards.

When flying with the wings level, moving the control column to the left will cause the left aileron to go up and the right aileron to go down. This causes the left wing to go down and the glider "rolls" *(or "banks")* to the left. This banking of the wings is what causes the glider to turn – in this case to the left.

Moving the control column to the right will cause the right aileron to go up and the left aileron to go down. This causes the right wing to go down and the glider rolls *(or banks)* to the right. This would cause the glider to turn to the right.

View over the Nose
Wings Level

Note: the horizon is symmetrical with cockpit edge.

Move Control Column to
Left

Left wing goes down, glider starts to turn left, horizon appears at an angle.

Move Control Column to
Right

Right wing goes down, glider starts to turn right, horizon appears at an angle.

The Rudder

The rudder is a vertical control surface attached by hinges to the rear of the glider's fin. It is connected by cables to two pedals in the cockpit.

Pushing on the left pedal moves the rudder to the left. This swings the glider's nose to the left.

Pushing on the right rudder pedal moves the rudder to the right. This swings the glider's nose to the right.

However, it is the banking of the glider with the ailerons which actually turns the glider – so don't confuse the swinging of the nose with rudder as turning the glider. Unlike on a boat, the rudder does not turn the glider. So why have a rudder? It is used in conjunction with the ailerons to make the glider turn more smoothly and efficiently.

Turning the Glider

Lookout

The first thing that your instructor will stress before the turn is started is the need to maintain a really good **LOOKOUT**. There are often many other gliders flying from the same site, as well as other types of aircraft passing through the area in which you are flying. So safety depends on every pilot keeping his or her eyes open for any other aircraft. You will be encouraged to tell your instructor if you see another glider or aeroplane in the vicinity.

Before starting a turn make sure you have a look all around the area – not just in the direction in which you are going to turn. If it is clear, you can begin the turn. At this point it is best to look straight ahead over the nose of the glider, as this will give you the best indication of how the turn is progressing.

Starting the Turn

To turn the glider to the left, move the control column to the left and at the same time push forward on the left rudder pedal. The glider will bank to the left and the glider will start to turn. A slight backward movement of the control column is usually required to prevent the nose from lowering and the speed increasing.

Once you have enough bank, move the control column to a position just right of centre and reduce the amount of rudder. The glider will now be in a turn.

Exiting the Turn

To stop the glider turning to the left, move the control column more to the right at the same time as pushing on the right rudder pedal. When the wings are level, centralise the control column and the rudder pedals. You might have to relax any back-pressure you had applied on the control column to keep the correct nose attitude.

The glider will now have stopped turning.

To turn to the right use the same technique but start with moving the controls to the right. Control movements to the left will be required to exit the turn.

After your Glider Trial Flight

So after you have had your Glider Trial Flight, and most likely enjoyed the experience, you might want learn a bit more about gliding or even take up the sport. If so, you need to know how to go about it.

Your instructor and other club members will certainly be good sources of information. They will be able to give you a lot of useful details about the local club. Until you get the chance to make such enquiries, the following notes describe some of the options available at many gliding clubs.

Club Membership

In order to fly from a gliding club, you will have to become a member of the club. Membership fees vary from club to club and usually reflect the size of the club and the facilities available. However, the chances are that your Glider Trial Flight arrangement entitled you to a membership for a limited time – typically 28 days.

It may even be that joining the club soon after having a Glider Trial Flight will result in some reduction of the initial membership fee. Such deals vary, depending on the club.

There may also be a "one off" joining fee in addition to the annual membership fee.

The cost of the actual flying as a club member is not unreasonable and reflects the operating costs of the gliding club.

Normally, the cost of a flight is broken into two elements: the launch fee and the hire of the glider. Launching will cost more if launched behind a light aircraft than it would if the launch is by winch or car launch.

When training, normally there is no charge for the instructor's time.

Continuing your Training

Let's not forget that your Glider Trial Flight was your first instructional flight in the glider. In other words, your training has begun. So should you decide to continue to learn to fly a glider, it is simply a matter of taking more instructional flights. There may be several options open to you to help you achieve this.

Having joined a gliding club, you can simply turn up and fly as a club member. This usually involves turning up early in the day and placing your name on a list along with other students wanting instruction. Students fly on a *"first come - first served"* **basis.**

Some clubs run training courses. These normally limit the number of students per instructor and are an excellent way to maintain consistency in your training. These courses can vary considerably in the way they are organised.

Some clubs run 5-day residential courses that include all costs. There are also weekend courses, which may be run along the same lines or where you pay for the flying as you go.

There are one-day courses and evening courses where the same group of students and instructors meet to fly on the same evening each week throughout the season.

After your Glider Trial Flight, ask about these and the other options for continuing your training.

Where does the Training Lead?

Once your instructor feels you are ready, and all of the training exercises have been completed satisfactorily, you will be allowed to take the glider for a flight on your own; that is, you will fly "solo". This is the initial aim of all trainee pilots and is a great personal moment that every pilot remembers with pride.

This huge step – the first time you have flown a glider on your own - is only your first step to becoming not just a glider pilot, but a **SOARING PILOT**.

Once you can fly the glider safely, you will learn to use rising air currents to fly higher, across country and to stay in the air for hours on end. While gaining these skills you will have many hours of pleasure, all of which started with your Glider Trial Flight.

BRITISH GLIDING ASSOCIATION

Kimberley House

Vaughan Way

Leicester LE1 4SE

Telephone 0116 2531051

Website: www.gliding.co.uk

Email: bga@gliding.co.uk

The following is a list of some of the larger gliding clubs in the various regions of the UK. There are many more throughout the country. To find other clubs – perhaps closer to where you live – a complete list of clubs and contact numbers is available from the British Gliding Association.

BOOKER GLIDING CLUB

Wycombe Air Park

Marlow

Bucks

SL7 3DR

Tel: 01494 442501

Email: office@bookergc.nildram.co.uk

BRISTOL & GLOUCESTERSHIRE GLIDING CLUB

Nympsfield

Nr. Stonehouse

Gloucestershire

GL10 3TX

Email: secretary@bggc.demon.co.uk

Tel: 01453 860342

DERBYSHIRE & LANCASHIRE GLIDING CLUB

Camphill

Great Hucklow

Tideswell

Derbyshire SK17 8RQ

Tel: 01298 871270

Email: dlgc@gliding.u-net.com

DEVON & SOMERSET GLIDING CLUB

North Hill Airfield

Broadhembury

HONITON

Devon

Tel: 01404 841386

LASHAM GLIDING SOCIETY

Lasham Airfield

Lasham

ALTON

Hampshire GU34 5SS

Tel: 01256 384900

Email: office@lasham.org.uk

LONDON GLIDING CLUB

Tring Road

DUNSTABLE

Bedfordshire LU6 2JP

Tel: 01582 663419

Email: info@gliding.powernet.co.uk

MIDLAND GLIDING CLUB

The Long Mynd

CHURCH STRETTON

Shropshire SY6 6TA

Tel: 01588 650206

Email: office@longmynd.com

SCOTTISH GLIDING CENTRE

Portmoak Airfield

Scotlandwell by KINROSS

KY13 9JJ

Tel: 01592 840543

THE GLIDING CENTRE

Husbands Bosworth Airfield

LUTTERWORTH

Leicestershire LE17 6JJ

Tel: 01858 880521

Email: office@theglidingcentre.co.uk

ULSTER GLIDING CLUB

Bellarena

Seacoast Road

LIMAVADY

Co. Londonderry Tel: 028 7775 0301

YORKSHIRE GLIDING CLUB

Sutton Bank

THIRSK

North Yorkshire YO7 2EY

Tel: 01845 597237

Email: enquiry@ygc.co.uk

A First Class Starter Pack for the Glider Pilot

This pack contains the following items:

1. Glider Pilot's Manual
2. Meterology Simplifield
3. Pilot' s Weather
4. Glider Pilot's Log Book
5. Glider Pilot's Kneeboard
6. Flight Log
7. CAA Chart 1:250 000 *(your local area)*
8. Flight Bag

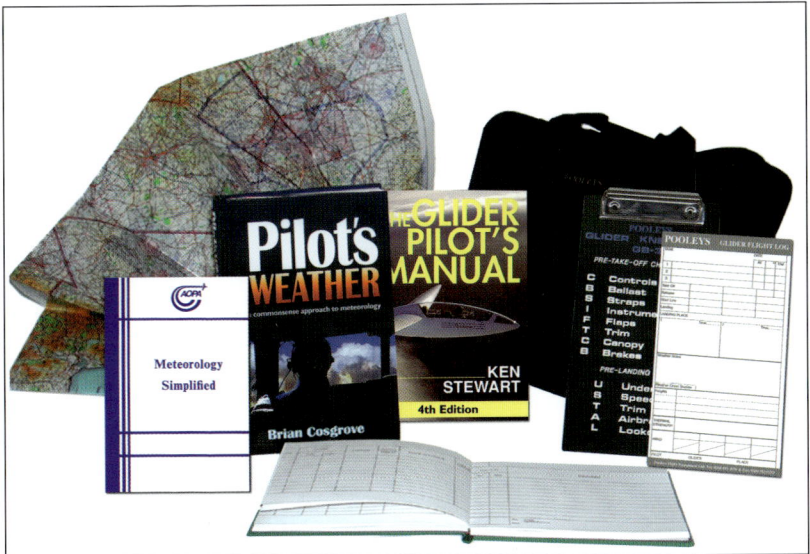

A	Alpha		**N**	November
B	Bravo		**O**	Oscar
C	Charlie		**P**	Papa
D	Delta		**Q**	Quebec
E	Echo		**R**	Romeo
F	Foxtrot		**S**	Sierra
G	Golf		**T**	Tango
H	Hotel		**U**	Uniform
I	India		**V**	Victor
J	Juliet		**W**	Whiskey
K	Kilo		**X**	X-Ray
L	Lima		**Y**	Yankee
M	Mike		**Z**	Zulu

Notes

Notes

Certificate of Completion
of a Glider

Trial Flying Lesson

This is to certify that

....

has completed an introductory flight in a glider and received
instruction in the operation of the glider's controls at:

....

....

Instructor (QFI) ....

Date ....